Is Christianity
Good
for the World?

Is CHRISTIANITY

GOOD

for the World?

ChristopherHITCHENS

DouglasWILSON

Cover design by David Dalbey.

This debate appeared originally in *Christianity Today,* and is reprinted in this format with permission.

A CIP catalogue record for this book is available from Library and Archives Canada

ISBN: 978-0-7710-4118-1

We acknowledge the financial support of the Government of Canada through the Book Publishing Industry Development Program and that of the Government of Ontario through the Ontario Media Development Corporation's Ontario Book Initiative. We further acknowledge the support of the Canada Council for the Arts and the Ontario Arts Council for our publishing program.

Printed and bound in the United States of America

McClelland & Stewart Ltd.
75 Sherbourne Street
Toronto, Ontario
M5A 2P9
www.mcclelland.com

2   3   4   5   12   11   10   09   08

CONTENTS

FOREWORD

by Jonah Goldberg

Douglas Wilson, a devout Christian, believes that Christianity is true and good. Christopher Hitchens, a no less devout atheist, believes Christianity is entirely untrue and ultimately not good. I fall somewhere in the murky middle, though I will confess my sympathies are more with Wilson, whom I do not know, than they are with Christopher, whom I consider a casual friend. As a non-Christian, I cannot claim that I believe that Christianity is unalloyed truth. As a fairly secular Jew who happens to believe in God as well as the positive role of both religion and Christianity, I'm undoubtedly ill-suited to adjudicate this thoughtful, passionate, and well-informed debate. Fortunately, that's not my assignment here. Rather, I'm simply here to get things started, to awaken the reader's palate for the meal ahead.

Christopher Hitchens is nothing if not an anti-totalitarian. As such, he sees his battle with religion as merely another front, or perhaps more precisely the central front, in his own very personal war on terror. His comparison of the Judeo-Christian God to *1984's* Big Brother is telling. In Orwell's dystopia men are told to worship their leader, Hitchens observes, and in the Old Testament they are told to worship the creator of the heavens. But the celestial Big Brother is even more oppressive than the man-made one. Whatever you make of the comparison, one might object that the relationship is more complicated than Hitchens suggests.

Voltaire's famous declaration (in a debate with an atheist, no less), "If God did not exist, it would be necessary to invent Him," gets close to the matter. Christopher would certainly dispute that God made us in his image, but he might well concede that men have a terrible habit of trying to remake themselves in the image of God. He would blame religion, at least in part, for this bloody habit. But the cruelest God-players, at least in the last century, have often been those most eager to destroy biblical religion and replace it with their own. The Jacobins were keen on bending what Robespierre correctly dubbed the "religious instinct" to their revolutionary needs. The Bolsheviks promised a "heaven on Earth." The Italian Fascists pursued the sacralization of politics. The Nazis sought to replace Christianity with a kind of pagan self-worship.

Wilson and Hitchens discuss the moral consequences of atheism with considerably more insight and sophistication than I could. But both men certainly agree that atheism doesn't require evil any more than faith alone bequeaths goodness. But it is worth pondering that Hitchens' quest for a religionless world of peace and comity is as utopian as the quest for universal Christian love. The yearning for *a* religious order is innate to mankind—even if some individual spiritual albinos find themselves missing the gene. Should Christopher succeed in burning Christianity to the ground, he will not be able to stop humanity from building a new temple in its place. And even if the proselytizers of the new faith call themselves atheists or worshippers of Reason, history shows that's no guarantee against industrial scale cruelty, inhumanity, and unthinking dogmatism.

Christianity's history is hardly unblemished, as Christopher Hitchens makes clear and Douglas Wilson concedes, but it does at least provide the resources for condemning those who do evil in its name. There are a great many "secular" *isms* that cannot make the same claim. They must—or choose to—simply redefine evil as disloyalty to the Cause, while any evil done to further the Cause is heroic. Christianity certainly had adherents who acted sinfully in God's name. But Christianity at least cultivates a moral imagination by which men can try to see their own actions through the eyes of a loving God. Given some of the alternatives, that hardly seems like the worst organizing principle for mankind.

Christopher of course rejects all of this. Christianity has good principles in it, he grudgingly concedes, but so do countless other systems and faiths. The Golden Rule is not God's but man's, and it has sprouted everywhere man has thrived, for man could not thrive without it. Hitchens has an excellent point there. And it is a point Wilson joy-fully tackles. As this is their debate, not mine, I should leave it to him to do exactly that.

But I should close by noting something that will be far more evident in the pages that follow than in the pages you've just read. This is a joyful book. Both men clearly love the subject, love wrestling with it and each other, and do so with an evident—and expressed—sense of gratitude. Whatever side of the debate you align your-self with, my guess is that you find that as refreshing as I do, given how joyless so much of the discourse on both sides of this debate tends to be. I salute both men for be-ing happy warriors in their respective causes and hope readers come away with a similar spirit (if Hitch will let me use that word).

Enjoy.

INTRODUCTION

by Christopher Hitchens

I had a long series of disagreements on a wide spectrum of questions with the late William F. Buckley, but there is a famous statement of his, much reprinted in the wake of his death, with which I am in almost complete agreement.

Here it is: I myself believe that the duel between Christianity and atheism is the most important in the world. I further believe that the struggle between individualism and collectivism is the same struggle reproduced on another level.

In order for me to be able to adopt this statement wholesale (it comes from Buckley's first book, *God and Man at Yale*) the word "Christianity" would have to be

replaced by the word "religion" and the struggle rede-
fined as one between liberty and totalitarianism.

Many of my exchanges with Douglas Wilson were
concerned with what I believe to be the falsity of the
metaphysical claims of religion, and also with what I regard as the emptiness of religion's claim to be the fount of
morality in our conduct. But I should not conceal the fact
that I am not so much an atheist as an *anti*-theist. I am,
in other words, not one of those unbelievers who wishes
that they had faith, or that they could believe. I am, rather, someone who is delighted that there is absolutely no
persuasive evidence for the existence of any of mankind's
many thousands of past and present deities.

It is to me an appalling thought that anyone could
wish for a supreme and absolute and unalterable ruler,
whose reign was eternal and unchallengeable, who required incessant propitiation, and who kept us all under
continual surveillance, waking and sleeping, which did
not even cease (and which indeed even intensified) after
our deaths. Such an awful system would mean that words
like "freedom" or terms like "free will" were devoid of
all meaning. This celestial Big Brother state would be the
last refinement of the totalitarian: it would hugely im-
prove on the hermetic and despotic state of *1984* in that
"thought-crimes"—offenses committed only in the imagination—would be detected at the instant they occurred.

Orwell's dystopian nightmare showed a state of affairs
where cruelty and power-worship were unapologetic
and conducted, so to say, for their own sake. But the
all-powerful regime demanded more than terrorized
obedience from its subjects. It also required of them that

they profess their *love* for Big Brother. It is this additional element in religious belief that I also find repellent to an extreme degree. One is quite literally *commanded* to love. And commanded not just to love others as much as oneself—a ridiculous and impossible injunction, as well as an internally contradictory one—but also to love a supreme being for whom one must simultaneously feel an overpowering fear. Countless central passages in Jewish and Christian and Muslim scripture drive home the critical point that god is not content with omnipotence and omniscience and omnipresence, but is jealous and demanding and impatient, and continually enraged with the built-in shortcomings with which he has deliberately lamed his creatures. Having been "created sick," in Fulke Greville's words, we are "commanded to be sound," and continuously and abjectly to "thank" a being who need not exert himself in the least to ensure that we live, suffer, and die. In the non-spiritual arena of life, power-relationships like this go under the general title of sado-masochism.

I suppose it can be objected that Jewish and Christian and Muslim dissidents have opposed real-world dictator-ships, often with great courage. But the point is not a very important one, and says nothing about the validity of the beliefs in question. After all, many Stalinists showed exemplary courage in resisting Hitler, and many anti-Semitic supporters of absolute monarchy in Russia put up a brave resistance to Communism. This doesn't alter the fact that they were opposing one tyranny with another. In any case, if religious resistance to oppression is to count as evidence, then so must religious collaboration with it, and indeed religious establishment of it. And of this, there is so much evidence that I need hardly detain the reader. The Catholic Church has to spend almost as much time in apologizing for its past crimes against humanity as it has to spend money on compensating the living victims of its rape-and-torture policy toward children. While if you glance at the Muslim world you will see that, without a single exception, the less pious a country is (Turkey, Indonesia, Tunisia) the better a chance it has of enjoying a semblance of democracy. The corollary holds with exactitude: the greater the strength of Islam's hold, the more terror and tyranny and misery is to be found. (Iran, the Taliban's Afghanistan, the prison-house of Saudi Arabia.)

So the original biblical myth probably contains an important kernel of moral truth to it. Having been created with a natural curiosity, the first man and his spouse are capriciously and nastily punished for the mere exercise of this indispensable faculty. There are those who claim to detect, in this positive action on their part, some sort of sin. There are also those who, for no reason that can be understood, regard us all as having been implicated in the said transgression, and as forever condemned to worm our way back into favor with a hard-to-please taskmaster. Spurning this as a sinister fairy-tale, I nonetheless point out that the very "first" recorded rebellion of the free intelligence was against the unreasonable dictates of religion, and will close by saying that this great tradition—which takes us from Democritus and Lucretius through Galileo and Spinoza and Voltaire and all the way to Darwin and Einstein—is the record of humanity's triumph over barbaric theocracy and its scriptural guidebook. There is more beauty and symmetry in this achievement—and more genuine brotherly love— than in any invocation of the absent dimension of the supernatural.

INTRODUCTION

by Douglas Wilson

God knew that we were going to need to pick up dimes, and so He gave us fingernails. He knew that twilights displayed in blue, apricot, and battle gray would be entirely astonishing and beyond us, and so He gave us eyes that can see in *color*. He could have made all food quite nourishing, but which tasted like wadded up newspaper soaked in machine oil. Instead He gave us the tastes of watermelon, pecans, oatmeal stout, buttered corn, apples, fresh bread, grilled sirloin, and twenty-five-year-old scotch. And He of course knew that we were going to need to thank Him, and so He gave us hearts and minds.

The issue of thanksgiving is really central to the whole debate about the existence of God. On the one hand, if there is no God, there is no need to thank anyone. We are here as the result of a long chain of impersonal processes, grinding their way down to our brief moment in time. If there is a God, then every breath, every moment, every sight and sound, is sheer, unadulterated *gift*. And, as our mothers taught us, when someone gives you presents like this, the only appropriate response is to thank them.

The apostle Paul places this matter of thanksgiving right at the center of man's relationship to God. When he describes those who would live their lives without God, he identifies two problems they have. The first is that they cannot handle the Godness of God, and the second is that they do not want to thank Him. He says, "Because that, when they knew God, they glorified him not as God, neither were thankful; but became vain in their imaginations" (Rom. 1:21). They did not glorify Him as God, and they were not thankful to Him. The result of these two problems together is that their imagination and thought processes are overtaken by vanity.

Anticipating a response that Christopher Hitchens might make to this, saying that this is just an *ad hominem* attack, I grant that Paul does goes on to say that "professing to be wise, they became fools." But this biblical use of that word *fool* is often misunderstood and misapplied (see also Ps. 14:1). The apostle does not say "professing to be wise, they became idiots and dolts." The issue is not one of intelligence, or intellectual rpm. If it were, I for one would be careful to stay out of debates with Christopher Hitchens. But a superb engine with over 350 horsepower will not do anything for the car if the clutch is not let out. And if the clutch is engaged, a small riding lawn mower can scoot across the lawn like anything. In case the metaphor is too obscure, admitting that God is God and rendering thanks to Him is the only thing that can let the clutch out.

As the reader picks up this small volume, I would ask him to read it with the ancient triad of truth, goodness and beauty in mind. On each of these topics I want the reader to ask what it might mean if there is no God, and in addition to ask what it means for the verbal tools that Christopher Hitchens routinely employs. My argument does not focus so much as a challenge to what Christopher Hitchens wants to reject (God) as what he still desires to keep regardless. He has chopped down the tree and yet still wants the fruit to be there at harvest. He has banished apples trees from his yard, but still wants the apple pies. Christopher Hitchens argues carefully, but given atheism, I want him to justify his use of reason. If there is no God, what is truth? Christopher Hitchens displays great moral indignation, but, given atheism, I want him to justify that indignation. If there is no God, then who cares? And Christopher Hitchens writes as a very capable wordsmith, but given atheism, I want him to justify his vibrant and engaging prose. If there is no God, then yammer, yamber, yaw&^% . . .

And last, since I have been talking so much about gratitude, it is important for me to note some of my obligations here. I am of course grateful to God for the opportunity to engage with an atheist of Christopher Hitchens' caliber. I am also grateful to Christopher himself (may I call you Christopher?) for his gentlemanly cooperation behind the scenes, and his willingness to go at it bare-knuckled in the ring. I am thankful to Aaron Rench, my agent, for setting this whole thing up, and to *Christianity Today Online* for agreeing to publish the initial debate. And of course I am grateful to Lucy Jones and the entire gang at Canon Press for their work to publish this exchange in this format.

ROUND

1

HITCHENS to WILSON

In considering the question at hand (for which my thanks are due to your generosity and hospitality in inviting my response), I have complete confidence in replying in the negative. This is for the following reasons.

[1] Although Christianity is often credited (or credits itself) with spreading moral precepts such as "Love thy neighbor," I know of no evidence that such precepts derive from Christianity. To take one instance from each Testament, I cannot believe that the followers of Moses had been indifferent to murder and theft and perjury until they arrived at Sinai, and I notice that the parable of the good Samaritan is told of someone who by definition cannot have been a Christian.

To these obvious points, I add that the "Golden Rule" is much older than any monotheism, and that no human society would have been possible or even thinkable without elementary solidarity (which also allows for self-interest) between its members. Though it is not strictly relevant to the ethical dimension, I would further say that neither the fable of Moses nor the wildly discrepant Gospel accounts of Jesus of Nazareth may claim the virtue of being historically true. I am aware that many Christians also doubt the literal truth of the tales but this seems to me to be a problem for them rather than a difficulty for me. Even if I accepted that Jesus—like almost every other prophet on record—was born of a virgin, I cannot think that this proves the divinity of his father or the truth of his teachings. The same would be true if I accepted that he had been resurrected. There are too many resurrections in the New Testament for me to put my trust in any one of them, let alone to employ them as a basis for something as integral to me as my morality.

[2] Many of the teachings of Christianity are, as well as being incredible and mythical, immoral. I would principally wish to cite the concept of vicarious redemption, whereby one's own responsibilities can be flung onto a scapegoat and thereby taken away. In my book, I argue that I can pay your debt or even take your place in prison but I cannot absolve you of what you actually did. This exorbitant fantasy of "forgiveness" is unfortunately matched by an equally extreme admonition—which is that the refusal to accept such a sublime offer may be punishable by eternal damnation. Not even the Old Testament, which speaks hotly in recommending

genocide, slavery, genital mutilation, and other horrors, stoops to mention the torture of the dead. Those who tell this evil story to small children are not damned by me, but have been damned by history and should also be condemned by those who shrink from cruelty to children (a moral essential that underlies all cultures).

The late C.S. Lewis helps make this point for me by emphasizing that the teachings of Jesus only make sense if the speaker is the herald of an imminent kingdom of heaven. Otherwise, would it not be morally unsafe to denounce thrift, family, and the "taking of thought for the morrow"? Some of your readers may believe that this teaching is either true—in the sense of an imminent redemption—or moral. I believe that they would have a difficult time believing both things at once, and I notice the futility as well as the excessive strenuousness (sometimes called "fanaticism" in tribute to the way that the two things pull in opposite directions) of their efforts. Another way of phrasing this would be to say that if Christianity was going to save us by its teachings, it would have had to perform better by now. And so to my succeeding point.

[3] If Christianity is to claim credit for the work of outstanding Christians or for the labors of famous charities, then it must in all honesty accept responsibility for the opposite. I shall not condescend to your readers in specifying what these "opposites" are, but I suggest once more that you pay attention to the Golden Rule. If hymns and psalms were sung to sanctify slavery—just to take a recent example—and then sung by abolitionists, then surely the non-fanatical explanation is that morality

requires no supernatural sanction? Every Christian church has had to make some apology for its role in the Crusades, slavery, anti-Semitism, and much else. I do not think that such humility discredits faith as such, because I tend to think that faith is a problem to begin with, but I do think that humility will lead to the necessary conclusion that religion is man-made.

On the other hand from humility, the fantastic idea that the cosmos was made with man in mind strikes me as the highest form of arrogant self-centeredness. And this brings me to what must be (within the limits of this short essay) my closing point. We are not without knowledge on these points, and the boundaries are being expanded at a rate which astonishes even those who do not look for a single cause of such vast and diverse phenomena. There is more awe and more reverence to be derived from a study of the heavens or of our DNA than can be found in any book written by a fearful committee in the age of myth (when Aquinas took astrology seriously and Augustine invented "limbo").

I cannot, of course, prove that there is no supervising deity who invigilates my every moment and who will pursue me even after I am dead. (I can only be happy that there is no evidence for such a ghastly idea, which would resemble a celestial North Korea in which liberty was not just impossible but inconceivable.) But nor has any theologian ever demonstrated the contrary. This would perhaps make the believer and the doubter equal—except that the believer claims to know, not just that God exists, but that his most detailed wishes are not merely knowable but actually known. Since religion drew its first breath when the species lived in utter ignorance and considerable fear, I hope I may be forgiven for declining to believe that another human being can tell me what to do, in the most intimate details of my life and mind, and to further dictate these terms as if acting as proxy for a supernatural entity. This tyrannical idea is very much older than Christianity, of course, but I do sometimes think that Christians have less excuse for believing, let alone wishing, that such a horrible thing could be true. Perhaps your response will make me reconsider?

WILSON to HITCHENS

I want to begin by thanking you for agreeing to—as the diplomats might put it—a "frank exchange of views." And I certainly want to thank the folks at *Christianity Today* for hosting us.

P.G. Wodehouse once said that some minds are like soup in a poor restaurant—better left unstirred. I am afraid that I find myself sympathizing with him as I consider atheism. I had been minding my own business on this subject for a number of years when I saw Sam Harris's book on the desk of a colleague, and that led to my book in response, not to mention a review of Richard Dawkins's most recent book, and now a series of responses to your *God is Not Great,* all culminating in this exchange. I am afraid that my problem is this: The more I stir the bowl, the more certain fumes, mystery meats, and questions keep floating to the surface. Here are a few of them.

Your first point was that the Christian faith cannot credit itself for all that "Love your neighbor" stuff, not to mention the Golden Rule, and the reason for this is that such moral precepts have been self-evident to everybody throughout history who wanted to have a stable society. You then move on to the second point, which contains the idea that the teachings of Christianity are "incredibly immoral." In your book, you make the same point about other religions. Apparently, basic morality is *not* all that self-evident. So my first question is: Which way do you want to argue this? Do all human societies have a grasp of basic morality, which is the theme of your first point, or has religion poisoned *everything*, which is the thesis of your book?

The second thing to observe in this regard is that Christians actually do not claim that the gospel has made the world better by bringing us turbo-charged ethical information. There *have* been ethical advances that are due to the propagation of the faith, but that is not where the action is. Christians believe—as C.S. Lewis argued in *The Abolition of Man*—that nonbelievers do understand the basics of morality. Paul the apostle refers to the Gentiles, who did not have the law but who nevertheless knew by nature some of the tenets of the law (Rom. 2:14). But the world is not made better because people can understand the ways in which they are being bad. It has to be made better by Good News—we must receive the gift of forgiveness and the resultant ability to live more in conformity to a standard we already knew (but were necessarily failing to meet). So the gospel does not consist of new and improved law. The gospel makes the world better through Good News, not through guilt trips or good advice.

In your second objection, you gaily dismiss the Old Testament, "which speaks hotly in recommending genocide, slavery, genital mutilation, and other horrors." Setting aside for the moment whether your representation of the Old Testament is judicious or accurate, let me assume for the sake of discussion that you have accurately summarized the essence of Mosaic ethics here. You then go on to say that we who teach such stories to children have been "damned by history." But why should this "damnation by history" *matter* to any of us reading Bible stories to kids, or for that matter, to any of the people who did any of these atrocious things, on *your* principles? These people are all dead now, and we who read the stories are all going to be dead. Why should any of us care about the effeminate judgments of history? *Should* the propagators of these "horrors" have cared? There is no God, right? Because there is no God, this means that—you know—genocides just happen, like earthquakes and eclipses. It is all matter in motion, and these things happen.

If you are on the receiving end, there is only death, and if you are an agent delivering this genocide, the long-term result is brief victory and death at the end. So who cares? Picture an Israelite during the conquest of Canaan, doing every bad thing that you say was occurring back then. During one of his outrages, sword above his head, should he have stopped for a moment to reflect on the possibility that you might be right? "You know, in about three and a half millennia, the consensus among historians will be that I am being bad right now. But if there is no God, this disapproval will certainly not disturb my oblivion. On with the rapine and slaughter!" On *your* principles, why *should* he care?

In your third objection, you say that if "Christianity is to claim credit for the work of outstanding Christians or for the labors of famous charities, then it must in all honesty accept responsibility for the opposite." In short, if we point to our saints, you are going to demand that we point also to our charlatans, persecutors, shysters, slave-traders, inquisitors, hucksters, televangelists, and so on. Now allow me the privilege of pointing out the structure of your argument here. If a professor takes credit for the student who mastered the material, aced his finals, and went on to a career that was a benefit to himself and the university he graduated from, the professor must (fair-ness dictates) be upbraided for the dope-smoking slacker that he kicked out of class in the second week. They were both formally enrolled, is that not correct? They were both *students,* were they not?

What you are doing is saying that Christianity must be judged not only on the basis of those who believe the gospel in truth and live accordingly but also on the ba-sis of those baptized Christians who cannot listen to the Sermon on the Mount without a horse laugh and a life to match. You are saying that those who excel in the course and those who flunk out of it are all the same. This seems to me to be a curious way of proceeding.

You conclude by objecting to the sovereignty of God, saying that the idea makes the whole world into a ghastly totalitarian state, where believers say that God (and who does He think *He* is?) runs everything. I would urge you to set aside for a moment the theology of the thing and try to summon up some gratitude for those who built our institutions of liberty. Many of them were actually inspired by the idea that since God is exhaustively sovereign, and because man is a sinner, it follows that all earthly power must be limited and bounded. The idea of checks and balances came from a worldview that you dismiss as inherently totalitarian. Why did those societies where this kind of theology predominated produce, as a direct result, our institutions of civil liberty?

One last question: In your concluding paragraph you make a great deal out of your individualism and your right to be left alone with the "most intimate details of [your] life and mind." Given your atheism, what account are you able to give that would require us to respect the individual? How does this individualism of yours flow from the premises of atheism? Why should anyone in the outside world respect the details of your thought life any more than they respect the internal churnings of any other given chemical reaction? That's all our thoughts are, isn't that right? Or, if there is a distinction, could you show how the premises of your atheism might produce such a distinction?

HITCHENS to WILSON

This is mildly amusing casuistry which—aside from its recommendation of Wodehouse—contains nothing that distinguishes it from Islam or Hinduism or indeed humanism. Were I a Christian, I would be highly unsettled by the huge number of concessions that Wilson makes. Since I am not a Christian, I mutter a mild "thank you" for his admission that morality has nothing at all to do with the supernatural. My book argues that religious belief has now become purely optional and cannot be mandated by anything revealed or anything divine. It is one among an infinite number of private "faiths," which do not disturb me in the least as long as its adherents agree to leave me alone.

Since Wilson does not even attempt to persuade me that Christ died for my sins (and can yet vicariously forgive them) or that I am the object of a divine design or that any of the events described in the two Testaments actually occurred or that extreme penalties will attend any disagreement with his view, I am happy to leave our disagreement exactly where it is: as one of the decreasingly interesting disputes between those who cling so tentatively to man-made "Holy Writ" and those who have no need to consult such texts in pursuit of truth or beauty or an ethical life. The existence or otherwise of an indifferent cosmos (the overwhelmingly probable state of the case) would no more reduce our mutual human obligations than would the quite weird theory of a celestial dictatorship, whether Aztec or Muslim or (as you seem to insist) Christian. The sole difference is that we would be acting out of obligation toward others out of mutual interest and sympathy but without the impulse of terrifying punishment or selfish reward. Some of us can handle this thought and some, evidently, cannot. I have a slight suspicion as to which is more moral.

On a recent visit to Arkansas, I ran into a huge billboard near the Little Rock airport which simply said "JESUS." This struck me as saying too much as well as too little, and I had almost forgotten it until Wilson's evasions brought it back to mind.

WILSON to HITCHENS

I am glad that you found my response mildly amusing. I am also grateful we share an appreciation for Wodehouse. And I am extremely glad that you would like me to begin talking about the death of Christ for sin—which I fully intend to do. But the pattern the New Testament gives us is to address the need for repentance first and *then* to talk about the need for faith in Christ as Savior. Within the boundaries of our discussion, repentance would be necessary because you have embraced the internal contradictions of atheism, all for the sake of avoiding God (Rom. 1:21; Ps. 14:1–2). So we *will* get to the gospel, but I am afraid I am going to have to ask you to hold your horses.

So, back to the business at hand, the business of intellectual repentance. Dismissing something as casuistry is not the same thing as a demonstration of casuistry, and refusing to answer questions because the *other* guy is being evasive is quite a neat trick . . . if you can pull it off.

I am afraid you misconstrued my acknowledgement that—with regard to public civic life—atheists can certainly behave in a moral manner. My acknowledgement was *not* that morality has nothing to do with the supernatural, as you represented, but rather that morality has nothing to do with the supernatural *if you want to be an inconsistent atheist*. Here is that point again, couched another way and tied into our topic of debate.

Among many other reasons, Christianity is good for the world because it makes hypocrisy a coherent concept. The Christian faith certainly condemns hypocrisy as such, but because there is a fixed standard, this makes it possible for sinners to fail to meet it or for flaming hypocrites to pretend that they are meeting it when they have no intention of doing so. Now my question for you is this: Is there such a thing as *atheist* hypocrisy? When another atheist makes different ethical choices than you do (as Stalin and Mao certainly did), is there an overarching common standard for all atheists that you are obeying and which they are not obeying? If so, what is that standard and what book did it come from? Why is it binding on them if they differ with you? And if there is not a common objective standard which binds all atheists, then would it not appear that the supernatural *is* necessary in order to have a standard of morality that can be reasonably articulated and defended?

So I am *not* saying you have to believe in the supernatural in order to live as a responsible citizen. I *am* saying you have to believe in the supernatural in order to be able to give a rational and coherent account of why you believe yourself obligated to live this way. In order to prove me wrong here, you must do more than employ words like "casuistry" or "evasions"—you simply need to provide that rational account. Given atheism, objective morality follows . . . how?

The Christian faith is good for the world because it provides the fixed standard which atheism cannot provide and because it provides forgiveness for sins, which atheism cannot provide either. We need the direction of the standard because we are confused sinners. We need the forgiveness because we are guilty sinners. Atheism not only keeps the guilt, but it also keeps the confusion.

ROUND
3

HITCHENS to WILSON

Here is a minor example of how the complacency of the religious allows them to be rude (and crude) in a manner which they might not so easily permit themselves in everyday discourse. I am quite familiar with the verse from the Psalms that describes me as a fool, and corrupt and abominable as well. (In my book, *God Is Not Great,* I point out that the psalmist was so delighted with this conceit that he reproduced it almost word for word at the opening of Psalm 53.) No great surprise—and no real offense taken—to find myself similarly dismissed as a dumb and vain ingrate in the epistle to the Romans. It's true that I never asked to be saved and don't want anyone to be martyred for me—or to martyr themselves against me, for that matter. All I ask of the apostle Paul is that he and his followers and emulators leave me alone.

On the much more pertinent question of the origin of ethical imperatives, which I believe to be derived from innate human solidarity and not from the supernatural, let me likewise offer an instance from each Testament. Let us assume that the tales can be taken at face value. Is it to be believed that the Jews got as far as Sinai under the impression that murder, theft, and perjury were more or less all right? And, in the story of the good man from Samaria, is it claimed that the man went out of his way to help a fellow creature because of a divine instruction? He was clearly, since he preceded Jesus, not motivated by Christian teaching. And if he was a pious Jew, as seems probable, he would have had religious warrant and authority NOT to do what he did, if the poor sufferer was a non-Jew. It is belief in the supernatural that can make otherwise decent people do things that they would otherwise shrink from—such as mutilating the genitals of children, frightening infants with talk of hellfire, forbidding normal sexual practices, blaming all Jews for "deicide," applauding suicide-murderers, and treating women as Paul or Muhammad thought they should be treated.

I have nowhere claimed nor even implied that unbelief is a guarantee of good conduct or even an indicator of it. (I have sometimes thought that atheists have a slight superiority in one respect, in that we come to our conclusions without any element of self-centered wish-thinking about death.) But an atheist can as easily be a nihilist, a sadist—even a casuist.

On the matter of Stalin and the related question of secular or atheist barbarism, I shyly call your attention to chapter seventeen of my little book, which attempts an answer to this frequently asked question. Until 1917, Russia had been ruled for centuries by an absolute monarch who was also the head of a corrupt and bigoted Orthodox Church and was supposed to possess powers somewhat more than merely human. With millions of hungry and anxious people so long stultified and so credulous, Stalin the ex-seminarian would have been a fool if he did not call upon such a reservoir of ignorance and servility, and seek to emulate his predecessor. If Mr. Wilson would prefer to compare like with like and point to a society that lapsed into misery and despotism by following the precepts of Epicurus or Spinoza or Jefferson or Einstein, I will gladly meet him on that ground.

WILSON to HITCHENS

There are a few slight confusions that I would like deal with briefly within the scope of my first few paragraphs. Weather permitting, I would then like to take just a short space to address the central point which you have (again) missed. The remainder of my time will be spent on your claim concerning the origin of ethical imperatives. I would like to do all this in order to set the stage for our unfolding discussion of the central reason why Christianity is good for the world—it is good for the world because Jesus died for the life of the world.

First, the confusions. The point of citing Psalm 14:1 was not to infer that I thought you were "dumb." In the wisdom literature of the Old Testament, folly is a moral question, not a matter of intelligence. I am quite prepared to cheerfully grant (and not for the sake of the argument) that you are my intellectual superior. But our discussion is not about who has more horsepower under his intellectual hood—the point of discussion is whether your superior car is on the right road. A fast car can be a real detriment on a dark night when the bridge is out. And you insist on continuing to wear the sunglasses of atheism.

Now the second confusion concerns your citation of the parable of the Good Samaritan. The popular name for the parable should have been a giveaway—you acknowledge that the protagonist of the story was "from Samaria," but you miss that this was an ethnic and racial issue and not a question of where he happened to live. The man beat up by the side of the road was a Jew, the priest and Levite who passed by on the other side were Jews, and the man who stopped was a despised half-breed, a Samaritan. But you say that it was probable that the Samaritan was a Jew, which inverts the whole story and indicates to me that you have not really been reading the text very closely (Lk. 10:27–37). But to answer your point in even bringing the story up, the Samaritan did not need the teaching of Jesus to do what God desired here. Jesus cited the story as an exposition of the second greatest commandment, which is to love your neighbor as yourself. A certain lawyer had asked Jesus to "define neighbor" in order to justify himself, and Jesus then told this story to illustrate the point of an ancient law. So the duty to love our neighbor was revealed to Old Testament writers about a millennium and a half before the Samaritan fulfilled it in his charitable act.

You say, incidentally, that this kind of law was bringing coals to Newcastle—Moses came down from the mount and told people that murder, theft, and perjury were wrong, and all the assembled rolled their collective eyes. "We already knew that!" But the problem is that ancient man didn't know that, and modern man still doesn't know it. To state some of the issues that are subsumed under just one of the three categories you mention is to point to controversies that continue down to this day. Consider some of the issues clustered under the easiest of these three to condemn—murder. We have abortion, infanticide, partial-birth abortion, euthanasia, genocide, stem-cell research, capital punishment, and unjust war. Murder is the big E on the eye chart, and we still can't see it that clearly.

Man, both ancient and modern, certainly knows the entire law of God if it is his own ox being gored, but the purpose of a law code is to have one standard in place for all parties when individuals want to set aside the standards of civilized life to suit themselves. And we need as much help with that as ancient man ever did.

Now we really need to address the point you continue to miss. I am not talking about whether atheists must do evil, or if they can do evil. I have denied the former, and you have now granted the latter. But that is not the point. We are not talking about whether your atheism compels you to run downtown this evening to shoot out the street lights. I grant that it does not. And we are not talking about whether atheists can do vile things. You grant that they can. We are talking about (or, more accurately, I am trying to talk about) whether or not atheism provides any rational basis for rational condemnation when others decide to misbehave this way. You keep saying, "I have come to my ethical position." I keep asking, "Yes, quite. But why did you do so?"

So the point is not whether we could rustle up some nice places governed by atheists or some hellholes governed by Christians. If given a choice between living in a Virginia governed by Jefferson and living in a Russia under the czars, I would opt to live under your beloved Jefferson. Fine. But this is not a concession, because it is not the point.

Take the vilest atheist you ever heard of. Imagine yourself sitting at his bedside shortly before he passes away. He says, following Sinatra, "I did it my way." And then he adds, chuckling, "Got away with it too." In our thought experiment, the one rule is that you must say something to him, and whatever you say, it must flow directly from your shared atheism—and it must challenge the morality of his choices. What can you possibly say? He did get away with it. There is a great deal of injustice behind him, which he perpetrated, and no justice in front of him. You have no basis for saying anything to him other than to point to your own set of personal prejudices and preferences. You mention this to him, and he shrugs. "Tomayto, tomahto."

I am certainly willing to take the same thought experiment. I can imagine some pretty vile Christians, and if I couldn't, I am sure you could help me. The difference between us is that I have a basis for condemning evil in its Christian guise. You have no basis for confronting evil in its atheist guise, or in its Christian guise, either. When you say that a certain practice is evil, you have to be prepared to tell us why it is evil. And this brings us to the last point—you make the first glimmer of an attempt to provide a basis for ethics.

You say in passing that ethical imperatives are "derived from innate human solidarity." A host of difficult questions immediately arise, which is perhaps why atheists are generally so coy about trying to answer this question. Derived by whom? Is this derivation authoritative? Do the rest of us ever get to vote on which derivations represent true, innate human solidarity? Do we ever get to vote on the authorized derivers? On what basis is innate human solidarity authoritative? If someone rejects innate human solidarity, are they being evil, or are they just a mutation in the inevitable changes that the evolutionary process requires? What is the precise nature of human solidarity? What is easier to read, the book of Romans or innate human solidarity? Are there different denominations that read the book of innate human solidarity differently? Which one is right? Who says?

And last, does innate human solidarity believe in God?

ROUND
4

HITCHENS to WILSON

Here is the reason why I lay so much stress in my book on the importance of William of Ockham and his justly celebrated razor. Why on earth—if you excuse the impression—do the faithful spend so much time creating a mystery where none exists? And why do they insist on inserting unwarrantable assumptions?

I take the plain meaning of the passage in Luke (in a section that is clotted with stories about the casting out of devils and other embarrassing sorceries) to be the duty to others in distress. Surely it loses much of its force if the lesson is about discrepant ethnicities of which we cannot in any case be certain? Nothing can "invert" the message to emulate the Samaritan and to go "and do thou likewise."

You dilute the purity of this—which is morally intel-
ligible to any atheist or humanist—by saying that there is
a millennium and a half delay between the "revelation"
of this simple act of charity and its anecdotal fulfillment.
You also appear to find no distinction between the in-
telligible injunction to "love thy neighbor" and the impossible order to love another "as thyself." We are not
so made as to love others as ourselves: This may admittedly be a fault in our "design," but in such a case the
irony would be at your expense. The Golden Rule is to
be found in the *Analects of Confucius* and in the motto
of the Babylonian Rabbi Hillel, who long predate the
Christian era and who sanely state that one should not
do to others anything that would be repulsive if done to
oneself. (Even this strikes me as either contradictory or
tautologous, since surely we agree that sociopaths and
psychopaths actually deserve to be treated in ways that
would be objectionable to a morally normal person.)

When you say that men have never known nor yet
understood the essential principle, however, you speak
absurdly. Ordinary morality is innate in my view. But if,
in yours, it is still not known, then centuries of divine
admonition have also gone to waste. You are trapped in
a net of your own making. Take a look at the list of actual or potential crimes that you mention. Genocide is
not condemned by the Old Testament and neither (as you
well know and have elsewhere conceded) is slavery. Rather, these two horrors are often positively recommended
by holy writ. Abortion is denounced in the Oath of Hip-
pocrates, which long predates Christianity. As for capital
punishment and unjust war, the secular and the religious

are alike at odds on the very definitions that underpin any condemnation. (When you include "stem-cell research," by the way, I assume that you unintentionally omitted the word "embryonic.")

To your needlessly convoluted subsequent question: Atheists are by no means "coy" on the question of evil or on the possibility of non-supernatural derivation of ethics. We are simply reluctant to say that, if religious faith falls—as we believe it must and to some extent already has—then the undergirding of decency falls also. And we do not fail to notice that a corollary is in play: The manner in which religion makes people behave worse than they might otherwise have done. Take a look at today's paper if you do not believe me: See what the parties of God are doing in Iraq. Or notice the sordid yet pious tradesmanship of Ralph Reed, Jack Abramoff, and the late Jerry Falwell. The latter's bedside is the one at which you should be asking your question—do you dare to say that a follower of Albert Einstein or Bertrand Russell would be gloating in the same way at their last hour? In either case—an atheist boaster and braggart or a hypocritical religious one—I trust that both of us would know enough to be quite "judgmental." I would differ from you only in not requiring any supernatural sanction or in claiming to be smug enough to possess such a power.

I am sorry to see that you sarcastically refer to Thomas Jefferson as "my" beloved. Do you not respect him also? And why can you not summon enough charity to believe that a non-believer can give blood, say, for no return, out of the sheer satisfaction of doing a service that involves only a benefit and no loss? According to you, my doing this is pointless unless I accept the incredible idea that, after hundreds of thousands of years of human life and suffering, God chose a moment a few thousand years ago to finally mount an intervention. You will have to accept sooner or later that a good person can be born who cannot force his mind to believe such a fantastic thing. At that point, you will see that your strenuous conditions are surplus to requirements.

In closing, I reply to your clumsy observation about my motor vehicle by citing Heine, who said:

> In dark ages people are best guided by religion, as in a pitch-black night a blind man is the best guide; he knows the roads and paths better than a man who can see. When daylight comes, however, it is foolish to use blind old men as guides.

The argument that you have been making was over long before either of us was born. There is no need for revelation to enforce morality, and the idea that good conduct needs a heavenly reward, or that bad conduct merits a hellish punishment, is a degradation of our right and duty to choose for ourselves.

WILSON to HITCHENS

You refer to the faithful "creating a mystery where none exists." May I get you to agree that the question "Why is there something here rather than nothing at all?" does not fall into that category? If you and I were standing on a little thought-experiment balcony watching either the moment when the cosmic boilers blew, giving us the Big Bang, or watching the first glorious creational response to God's *fiat lux,* can we agree that at that moment Ockham's razor would be of absolutely no use to either of us?

If Jesus had told a story about a black man stopping to help a beat-up white guy in Mississippi in the 1950's, and you retold the story later with the merciful one now suitably white, I think it would be appropriate for me to point out the inversion, and that the story had been significantly changed and *weakened.* And when I said that the Good Samaritan fulfilled an ancient law, I did not say that obedience to this law was dormant during the intervening time. Of course it was not. But neither was disobedience dormant, and Jesus was confronting a particular form of institutionalized disobedience—religious hypocrisy.

On the question of morality, you say that you are "simply reluctant" to say that if religious faith falls, then the undergirding decency must fall also. But your behavior goes far beyond a mere "reluctance to concede." Your book and your installments in this debate thus far are filled with fierce denunciations of various manifestations of immorality. You are playing Savonarola here, and I simply want to know the basis of your florid denunciations. You preach like some hot gospeler—with a floppy leather-bound book and all. I know the book is not the Bible and so all I want to know is what book it is, and why it has anything to do with me. Why should anyone listen to your jeremiads against weirdbeards in the Middle East or fundamentalist Baptists from Virginia like Falwell? On your terms, you are just a random collection of proto-plasm, noisier than most, but no more authoritative than any—which is to say, not at all.

You say that I need to admit that a "good person can be born" who can't get his mind around what I am saying about Jesus. But my initial claim has been far more modest. I am simply saying that a good person needs to be able, at a minimum, to define what goodness is and tell us what the basis for it is. Your handwaving—"ordinary morality is innate"—does not even begin to meet the standard.

There are three insurmountable problems for you here. The first is that *innate* is not a synonym for *authori-tative*. Why does anyone have to obey any particular prompting from within? And which internal prompt-ing is in charge of sorting out all the other competing promptings? Why? Second, the tangled skein of innate and conflicting moralities found within the billions of humans alive today also has to be sorted out and system-atized. Why do you get to do it and then come around and tell *us* how we must behave? Who died and left you king? And third, according to you, this innate morality of ours is found in a creature (mankind) that is a distant blood cousin of various bacteria, aquatic mammals, and colorful birds in the jungle. Your entire worldview has evolution as a key foundation stone, and evolution means nothing if not *change*. You believe that virtually every species has morphed out of another one. And when we change, as we must, all our innate morality changes with us, right? We have distant cousins where the mothers ate their young. Was that innate for them? Did they evolve out of it because it was evil for them to be doing that?

Now this is how all this relates to the assigned topic of our debate. We are asking if Christianity is good for the world. As a Christian discussing this with an atheist, I have sought to show in the first place that atheism has nothing whatever to say about this topic—one way or the other. If Christianity is bad for the world, atheists can't consistently point this out, having no fixed way of defining "bad." If Christianity is good for the world, atheists should not be asked about it either because they have no way of defining "good." Think of it as spiking your guns—so that I can talk about Jesus. And I want to do that because He is good for the world.

Jesus Christ is good for the world because He came as the life of the world. You point out, rightly, that loving our neighbor as we love ourselves is impossible for us, completely out of our reach. But you take this inability as a state of nature (which the commandment offends), while the Christian takes it as a state of death (which life offers to transform). Our complete inability to do what is right does not erase our obligation to do what is right. This is why the Bible describes the unbeliever as a slave to sin or one who is in a state of death. The point of each illustration is the utter and complete inability to do right. We were dead in our transgressions and sins, the apostle Paul tells us. So the death and resurrection of Christ are not presented by the gospel as medicine for everyone in the hospital, but rather as resurrection life in a cemetery.

The way of the world is to abide in an ongoing state of death—when it comes to selfishness, grasping, treachery, lust, hypocrisy, pride, and insolence, we consistently run a surplus. But in the death of Jesus that way of death was gloriously put to death. This is why Jesus said that when He was lifted up on the cross, He would draw all men to Himself. In the kindness of God, the Cross is an object of inexorable fascination to us. When men and women look to Him in His death, they come to life in His resurrection. And that is good for the world.

5

HITCHENS to WILSON

If you insist, I shall concede that the significance of the Samaritan lies in his ethnicity. It's not a very impressive parable to begin with, though when I was taught it first in Sunday school, it was held up as an example of universal charity (with the added implication, not strange to us for some reason, that pious people are no more likely to behave with love and compassion than are others). Incidentally, what do we know about the ethnicity of the man who fell among thieves, or of the tribal character of those thieves if it comes to that? Surely you should be able to pronounce with authority on those details, too?

I agree that the origins of the cosmos are obscure—mysterious, if you like—to both of us. It's still you who makes the mystery, though, by insisting that very recent developments on this tiny speck of a planet on the edge of a galaxy are what impart significance to the entire "Big Bang" or divine first cause. To ask what caused either is to invite, as you are aware, an infinite regression of questions about what caused either of those causes. In my book I cite the great [Pierre-Simon, Marquis de] LaPlace, who opened the modern era by saying that accounts of the cosmos and its workings were now complete, or incomplete, on their own terms. They did not require a "god." Belief in a deity has been optional ever since. Believe it if you choose, but be aware that it raises more questions than it answers (actually it doesn't answer any important questions) and is thus highly vulnerable to Ockham's trusty edge. Deists used to agree with you about a Creator but were not religious in that the assumption of such an entity did not license the further assumption that he or she desired to intervene in human affairs, let alone the assumption that the torture and death of a single individual in a backward part of the Middle East was the solution that we had been awaiting for tens of thousands of years of brutish *homo sapiens* existence.

Apply something of the same reasoning to the origins of morality. I say that our "innate" predisposition to both good and wicked behavior is precisely what one would expect to find of a recently-evolved species that is (as we now know from the study of DNA) half a chromosome away from chimpanzees. By the way, do not take that as a denigration of humankind. Primate and elephant and even pig societies show considerable evidence of care for others, parent-child bonding, solidarity in the face of danger, and so on. As Darwin put it:

> Any animal whatever, endowed with well-marked social instincts, the parental and filial affections being here included, would inevitably acquire a moral sense or conscience, as soon as its intellectual powers had become as well-developed, or nearly as well-developed, as in man.

We can now observe this to be the case. But animal and human "altruism" is contradicted by the way in which species are also designed to fight with, kill, dominate, and even consume each other. Humans are capable of even greater cruelty because only they have the imagination to inflict it. I do not think that this indicts the Creator who made them this way, because I long ago dispensed with the assumption that there is any such entity. Thus, it is you and not I who are left with the questions about God's coexistence with evil. See where your talent for needless complexity has left you.

The fluctuations between social and anti-social conduct are fairly consistent across time and space: some societies have licensed cannibalism but they tend to die out, and others have licensed human sacrifice and infanticide (usually under the influence of some priesthood). But I answer your question by making the pragmatic observation that, if we surrendered to our lower instincts all the time, there would be no language in which to write this argument between us and no society in which we could find an audience. The struggle to assert what is positive in our human capacity—I don't mind Lincoln's metaphor of our "better angels" if you promise not to take it too literally—is arduous enough. If I take myself, I find that I can derive pleasure from giving blood for free and also from contemplating the deaths of my clerical-fascist enemies in the ranks of Al Qaeda and even from the misfortunes of others who do not threaten me. I am sure you could give parallel examples of your own. But telling us that we are created sick and then ordered to be well is no help in clarifying this problem. And telling us that the solution to it only became available some two thousand years ago, according to some highly discrepant and self-contradictory accounts, cannot strike me as anything but absurd. What on earth is proven—except your own vulnerability to making tautologous statements—by the claim that "Jesus Christ is good for the world because he came as the life of the world"? You cannot possibly "know" this. Nor can you present any evidence for it. And its corollary—that without Jesus we are abandoned to wickedness in all its forms—has the horrible implication that worthy actions are pointless unless accompanied by your own rather ill-grounded faith. As I say, believe it if it helps you. But do not insult the millions of people who have done the right thing without requiring any such supernatural authority. And do not tell me that I must be in love with death if I dissent from your view. That's too much. Your Christianity, in case you have not noticed, has actually made you a less compassionate and thoughtful person than, without its exorbitant presumptions, you would otherwise be.

WILSON to HITCHENS

I am afraid your argument is tangled up with greater difficulties than the ethnicity of the Samaritan, and so that issue really need not detain us any longer. I have been asking you to provide a *warrant* for morality, given atheism, and you have mostly responded with assertions that atheists can make what some people call moral choices. Well, sure. But what I have been after is what rational *warrant* they can give for calling one choice "moral" and another choice "not moral." You finally appealed to "innate human solidarity," a phrase that prompted a series of pointed questions from me. In response, you now tell us that we have an innate predisposition to *both* good and wicked behavior. But we are still stuck. What I want to know (*still*) is what warrant you have for calling some behaviors "good" and others "wicked." If both are innate, what distinguishes them? What could be wrong with just flipping a coin? With regard to your retort that my "talent for needless complexity" has simply gotten me "God's coexistence with evil," I reply that I would rather have my God *and* the problem of evil than your no God and "Evil? No problem!"

After this many installments, I now feel comfortable in asserting that I have posed this question to you from every point of the compass and have not yet received anything that approaches the semblance of an answer. On this question I am tempted to quote Wyatt Earp from the film *Tombstone*—"You gonna do something or just stand there and bleed?"—but I think I'll pass. Earp was not very much like the Good Samaritan.

But it is interesting that the same thing happens to you when you have to give some warrant for trusting in "reason." I noted your citation of LaPlace in your book and am glad you brought him up here. LaPlace believed he was not in need of the God hypothesis, just like you, but you should also know he held this position as a firm believer in celestial and terrestrial mechanics. He was a causal determinist, meaning that he believed that every element of the universe in the present was "the effect of its past and the cause of its future."

So if LaPlace is why you think belief in God is now "optional," this appeal of yours actually turns into quite a fun business. This doctrine means (although LaPlace admittedly got distracted before these implications caught up with him) that you, Christopher Hitchens, are *not* thinking your thoughts and writing them down because they are *true*, but rather because the position and velocity of all the atoms in the universe one hundred years ago necessitated it. And I am not sitting here thinking my Christian thoughts because they are the truth of God, but rather because that is what these assembled chemicals in my head always do in this condition and at this temperature. "LaPlace's demon" could have calculated and predicted your arguments (and word count) a century ago in just the same way that he could have calculated the water levels of the puddles in my driveway — and could have done so *using the same formulae*. This means that your arguments and my puddles are actually the same kind of thing. They are on the same level, so to speak.

If you were to take a bottle of Mountain Dew and another of Dr. Pepper, shake them vigorously, and put them on a table, it would not occur to anyone to ask which one is "winning the debate." They aren't debating; they are just fizzing. You refer to "language in which to write this argument," and you do so as though you believed in a universe where argument was a meaningful concept. Argument? *Argument?* I have no need for your "argument hypothesis." Just matter in motion, man.

You dismiss the idea that the death of Jesus—the "torture and death of a single individual in a backward part of the Middle East"—could possibly be the solution to the sorrows of our brutish existence. When I said that Jesus is good for the world because He is the life of the world, you just tossed this away. You said, "You cannot possibly 'know' this. Nor can you present any evidence for it."

Actually, I believe I can present evidence for what I know. But evidence comes to us like food, and that is why we say grace over it. And we are supposed to *eat* it, not push it around on the plate—and if we don't give thanks, it never tastes right. But here is some evidence for you, in no particular order. The engineering that went into ankles. The taste of beer. That Jesus rose from the dead on the third day, just like He said. A woman's neck. Bees fooling around in the flower bed. The ability of acorns to manufacture enormous oaks out of stuff they find in the air and dirt. Forgiveness of sin. Storms out of the North, the kind with lightning. Joyous laughter (diaphragm spasms to the atheistic materialist). The ocean at night with a full moon. Delta blues. The peacock that lives in my yard. Sunrise, in color. Baptizing babies. The pleasure of sneezing. Eye contact. Having your feet removed from

the miry clay, and established forever on the rock. You
may say none of this tastes right to you. But suppose you
were to bow your head and say grace over all of it. Try it
that way.

You say that you cannot believe that Christ's death
on the Cross was salvation for the world because the idea
is absurd. I have shown in various ways that absurdity
has not been a disqualifier for any number of your current
beliefs. You praise reason to the heights, yet will not give
reasons for your strident and inflexible moral judgments,
or why you have arbitrarily dubbed certain chemical processes "rational argument." That's absurd right *now,* and
yet there you are, holding it. So for you to refuse to accept
Christ because it is absurd is like a man at one end of the
pool refusing to move to the other end because he might
get wet. Given your premises, you will have to come up
with a different reason for rejecting Christ as you do.

But for you to make this move would reveal the two
fundamental tenets of *true* atheism. One: There is no
God. Two: I hate Him.

ROUND

6

HITCHENS to WILSON

Quo warranto is a very ancient question, meaning "by what right?" You ask me for my "warrant" for a code of right conduct and persist in mistaking my answer for an evasion. I in turn ask you by what right you assume that a celestial autocracy is a guarantee of morals, let alone by what right you choose your own (Christian) version of it as the only correct one. All deities have been hailed by their subjects as the fount of good behavior, just as they have been used as the excuse for inexcusable behavior.

My answer is the same as it was all along: Our morality evolved. Just as we have. Natural selection and trial-and-error have given us the vague yet grand conception of human rights and some but not yet all of the means of making these rights coherent and consistent. There is simply no need for the introduction of the extraneous or the supernatural. LaPlace was only one of those who concluded that religion is essentially irrelevant to important questions: an option if you choose it, but only one among many. (I have to say that your account of him makes him sound dangerously like the repulsive Calvin, but even the great Isaac Newton and the even greater Alfred Russell Wallace were prey to all kinds of superstitious delusions as they made their marvelous humanistic discoveries.)

There seems to be no easy way to discuss this other than in personal or individual terms. You and I have no idea what it is like to be a sociopath—someone who does not care about other people except inasmuch as they serve his turn—or a psychopath—someone who derives actual delight from inflicting misery on others. But we know that such people exist, and that they must be guarded against. I regard their existence as part of our haphazard evolution and our kinship with a nature that often favors the predator. You do not. Indeed, you apparently adopt the immoral and suicidal doctrine that advocates forgiveness for those who would destroy us. Please take care not to forgive my enemies, or the enemies of society. If I have to call such people "evil" (and I find I have no alternative), I do not deduce peaceful coexistence from that observation and do not want you being tender to them when it is my or my family's life that is at stake. God agrees.

Turning from this to the surprising amount of virtue that can be found in humans, I again choose not to confect a mystery where none exists. Leaving ordinary sins to one side—I do not steal other people's property, for example, and hope for a reciprocal restraint on their part, and do not pardon such offenses when they occur—I could mention something that is particular to our discussion. Every now and then, in argument, I find myself glib enough to make a cheap point or a point that might evoke instant applause from an audience. But I am always aware of doing so, or if you like, of the temptation to do so, and I strive (not always with success) to resist the tactic, and rather dislike myself when I give in to it. Why do I do this? Socrates called this restraint the *daemon*: an inner voice that helps us toward self-criticism. Many later thinkers have defined it in discrepant ways, but a definition is something short of an understanding.

I am content to regard it as indefinable, which is where we part company. My own inclination is to regard it as a human faculty without which we could not have—I shan't say "evolved" yet again—made the smallest progress as *homo sapiens*. You believe that I owe this inner prompting to the divine, and you further assert that a heavenly intervention made in the last two thousand years of human history (a microsecond of evolutionary time) is the seal on the deal. You will have to excuse me when I say that I think such a belief is, as well as incredible, immoral. It makes right action dependent on a highly improbable wager on the supernatural. To state the case in another way, it suggests that without celestial sanction, you yourself would be unrestrained in your appetites and careless of other people. Awful though many of your opinions are to me, I decline to believe that you would, if you lost your faith, become base and self-centered. It is, rather, religion that has made many morally normal people assent to appalling cruelties, including the mutilation of children's genitalia, the institution of slavery, the revulsion from female sexuality, and many other crimes from which an average infidel would, without any heavenly prompting, turn away. Ask yourself this question. Can you name one moral action, or moral utterance, performed or spoken by a believer that could not have been performed or spoken by an atheist? My email is available to any reader who is willing to accept this challenge.

I like your joke about the reduction of mirth to a spasm (there was a solemn critic of P.G. Wodehouse who defined the smile in terms of "naso-labial" contractions), but I think you let yourself down a bit with your Hallmark conclusion. I dare say that I could add to the list of joys and even include one or two subjects which Christianity and other religions have made difficult to discuss in public. However, I shall select my own recent investigation of my DNA, which can now be sequenced and analyzed. I was perfectly happy with the "revelation" of my own kinship with other species and quite overwhelmed by the skill and precision of those who allowed me to do it. A lot of wit and beauty and intelligence had to go into the confirmation of my status as an evolved animal, just as a great deal of dullness and stupidity is required for the continuing denial of it.

I think we shall do better if we do not resist evidence that may at first sight appear unwelcome or unsettling, just as we shall do better if we refuse conclusions for which there is no evidence at all.

WILSON to HITCHENS

Let me begin my final installment with my thanks to you for agreeing to this debate, as well as my thanks to *Christianity Today* for being such an amiable host.

Turning to our discussion, I would like to begin by noting several points of minor agreement. First, I do enjoy our shared appreciation of Wodehouse—although I have to say I was disappointed with your failure to pick up the Wodehousian echoes in my "Hallmark" conclusion.

Secondly, I quite agree with you that we ought not to "resist evidence that may at first sight appear unwelcome or unsettling." But this is not really a deep agreement, for we immediately go on to differ over which one of us is failing to honor this quite obvious principle. I have shown that you refuse to consider evidence for the fact that your assumption of what the universe actually *is* does not allow for valid descriptions of that universe to arise from within it. If one were to spill milk accidentally on the kitchen floor, and someone else came in and wanted to know what had happened, the one thing we can be sure of is that such an inquiring mind wouldn't ask the milk. The milk wouldn't know. *It's* the accident.

On the question of morality, you again attempt an answer: "My answer is the same as it was all along: Our morality evolved." There are two points to be made about this reply. The first concerns evolved morality and the *future*, and is a variation on my previous questions. If our morality evolved, then that means our morality *changes*. If evolution isn't done yet (and why should it be?), then that means our morality is involved in this on-going flux as well. And that means that everything we consider to be "moral" is really up for grabs. Our "vague yet grand conception of human rights" might flat disappear just like our gills did.

Our current "morals" are therefore just a way station on the road. No sense getting really attached to them, right? When I am traveling, I don't get attached to motel rooms. I don't weep when I have to part from them. So, in the future, after every ferocious moral denunciation you choose to offer your reading public, you really need to add something like, "But this is just a provisional judgment. Our perspective may evolve to an entirely different one some years hence," or "Provisional opinions only. Morality changes over time"—POOMCOT for short. It would look like this: "The Rev. Snoutworthy is an odious little toad, not to mention a waste of skin, and his proposal that we prosecute the brassiere editors of the Sears catalog on pornography and racketeering charges is an outrage against civilized humanity. But . . . POOMCOT."

This relates to the second point, which concerns evolved morality and the *past*. When dealing with people whose moral judgments have differed from yours, do you regard them as "immoral" or as "less evolved"? The rhetoric of your book, your tone in these exchanges, and your recent dancing on the grave of the late Jerry Falwell would all seem to indicate the former. In your choice of words, the people you denounce are to be *blamed*. The word *fulminations* comes to mind. You write like a witty but acerbic tenth-century archbishop with a bad case of the gout. But this is truly an odd thing to do if "morality" is a simple derivative of evolution. Are you filled with fierce indignation that the koala bear hasn't evolved ears that stick flat to the side of his head like they are supposed to? Are you wroth over the fact that clams don't have legs yet? When you notice that the bears at the zoo continue to suck on their paws, do you stop to remonstrate with them?

Your notion of morality, and the evolution it rode in on, can only concern itself with what *is*. But morality as Christians understand it, and the kind you *surreptitiously* draw upon, is concerned with *ought*. David Hume showed us that we cannot successfully derive *ought* from *is*. Have you discovered the error in his reasoning? It is clear from how you defend your ideas of "morality" that you have not done so. You are a gifted writer, and you have a flair for polemical voltage. But strip it all away, and what do you have underneath? You believe yourself to live in a universe where there is no such thing as any fixed *ought* or *ought not*. But God has gifted you with a remarkable ability to denounce what *ought not* to be. And so, because you reject Him, you have great sermons but no way of ever coming up with a text. When people start to notice the absence of texts, the absence of warrant, the absence of *reasons*, you adjust and compensate with rhetorical embellishment and empurpled prose. You are like the minister in the story who wrote in the margin of his notes, "Argument weak. Shout here."

Your invitation to us to try to "name one moral action . . . that could not have been performed or spoken by an atheist" shows that you continue to miss the point.

We have every reason to believe that such atheists, performing such deeds, will be as unable as you have been to give an account of *why* one deed should be seen as *good* and another as *evil*. You say you have no alternative but to call sociopaths and psychopaths "evil." But you surely do have an alternative. Why not just call them "different"?

A fixed standard, grounded in the character of God, allows us to define evil, but this brings with it the possibility of forgiveness. You reject forgiveness, but at the end of the day this means that you don't believe there is anything that needs forgiveness. This means you have destroyed the idea of evil, regardless of what you might "call" behaviors that happen to be inconvenient for you.

I noted from your book that you are a baptized Christian, so I want to conclude by calling and inviting you back to the terms of that baptism. Everyone who has been baptized into the name of the Father, Son, and Holy Spirit is carrying in their person the standing obligations of repentance, belief, and continued discipleship. Your Christian name *Christopher* means "bearer of Christ," your baptism means the same thing, and the Third Commandment requires you not to bear or carry that name in vain. Some, as you have done, revolt against the terms of this discipleship, but it does not mean that the demands of discipleship are somehow negated or revoked. I do not bring this up in order to upbraid you. I do not know if you departed from the faith because you drifted from it, bolted from it, or were chased out by hypocritical Christians. Regardless, the kindness of God is revealed to all of us in Christ, and everyone, whatever their story, has to come to terms with this kindness.

Jesus was not just one more character in history, however important—rather, He was and is the founder of a new history, a new humanity, a new way of being human. He was the last and true Adam. But before this new humanity in Christ could be established and begin its task of filling the earth, the old way of being human had to die. Before the meek could inherit the earth, the proud had to be evicted and sent away empty. That is the meaning of the Cross, the whole point of it. The Cross is God's merciful provision that executes autonomous pride and exalts humility. The first Adam received the fruit of death and disobedience from Eve in a garden of life; the true Adam bestowed the fruit of His life and resurrection on Mary Magdalene in a garden of death, a cemetery. The first Adam was put into the death of deep sleep and his wife was taken from his side; the true Adam died on the cross, a spear was thrust into His side, and His bride came forth in blood and water. The first Adam disobeyed at a tree; the true Adam obeyed on a tree. And everything is *necessarily* different.

Christ told His followers to tell everybody about this—about how the world is being moved from the old humanity to the new way of being human. Not only has the world been born again, so must *we* be born again. The Lord told us specifically to preach this Good News to every creature. He has established His great but welcoming household, and there is room enough for you. Nothing you have ever said or done will be held against you. Everything will be washed and forgiven. There is simple food—bread and wine—on the table. The door is open, and we'll leave the light on for you.